Celebrate Prayer
(Preschool)

Written by Mary Tucker

Illustrated by Carol Tiernon

Cover Illustrated by Kathryn Marlin

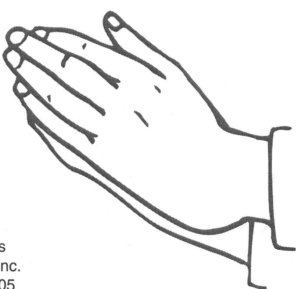

All rights reserved—Printed in the U.S.A.
Copyright © 1999 Shining Star Publications
A Division of Frank Schaffer Publications, Inc.
23740 Hawthorne Blvd., Torrance, CA 90505

Unless otherwise indicated, the New International Version of the Bible was used in preparing the activities in this book. Scripture taken from the HOLY BIBLE, NEW INTERNATIONAL VERSION. Copyright © 1973, 1978, 1984 International Bible Society. Used by permission of Zondervan Bible Publishers.

Table of Contents

To Parents and Teachers

Preschoolers love to pray, especially simple, memorized prayers. When questioned closely, it becomes apparent that children often repeat prayers they don't understand. It is important to teach children to pray, but it is even more important to help them understand what prayer is all about.

The activities in this book have been written to help 3- to 4-year-olds learn how to pray and understand simple prayers. They include crafts, dot-to-dots, mini books, coloring pictures, drawing, songs, games, and much more. (Two awards are also featured on page 48 and are a wonderful way to motivate children and praise their hard work.) The prayers and activities featured help the children realize that praying is much more than just saying some memorized words with their eyes closed. They will come to understand that prayer is talking to God, and they can talk to Him at any time, not just before meals or bedtime; they can talk to Him about anything; and they can pray wherever they are.

Some advance preparation, such as copying and cutting, is necessary for the crafts the children will make. Help them understand the purpose of each craft rather than just letting it be busy work. The materials you will need on hand are simple ones: construction paper, posterboard, scissors, glue, glitter, cotton balls, crayons, brad fasteners, tongue depressors, and yarn. Let the children do as much of the work for themselves as they can.

Also included to help children learn how to pray are Bible stories. Most should be familiar to the children, and each has been chosen because of its emphasis on prayer. Practice the stories before class so you can tell them smoothly, as much by memory as possible. Have your Bible open to the story you are telling even if you don't read from it. That way, the children will understand that the story comes from God's Word.

On pages 40–47 are some prayer poems and songs that are short and fairly easy for children to memorize. Of course, you'll need to repeat them several times, but preschoolers like repetition. (You'll get tired of them much sooner than they will!) Many of the prayers include simple actions for the children to do. Sometimes young children get so busy with the actions, they forget to talk or sing. Encourage them to do both.

As you teach the children about prayer, make sure you give them plenty of opportunities to actually pray. Give them practice in praying individually, silently, and as a group. You may want to send some of the prayer poems and songs home and encourage parents to say or sing the prayers with their children every day. You and the children will have a wonderful time as they begin to learn wonderful truths from God!

What Is Prayer?

Talk with the children about the meaning of prayer. Ask them the questions below, share the information with them, and let them share their ideas.

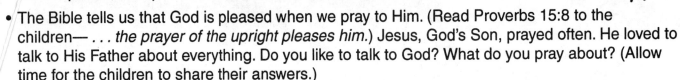

- How do you let your mom and dad or your friends know how you feel or what you want? (talk to them) God wants us to talk to Him, too. He wants us to tell Him everything. When we talk to God, we call it *prayer*.

- How is talking to God different from talking to Mom or Dad? (We can't see God.) In a way, praying is like talking to God on the telephone, except that He doesn't talk back to us out loud.

- The Bible tells us that God is pleased when we pray to Him. (Read Proverbs 15:8 to the children— . . . *the prayer of the upright pleases him.*) Jesus, God's Son, prayed often. He loved to talk to His Father about everything. Do you like to talk to God? What do you pray about? (Allow time for the children to share their answers.)

Teach the children the song below to help them learn all about prayer.

When I Pray
(Tune: "I Will Make You Fishers of Men")

When I pray, I'm talking to God,	(Fold hands, then point to heaven.)
Talking to God, talking to God.	(Point to heaven.)
When I pray, I'm talking to God,	(Fold hands, then point to heaven.)
And He hears my prayer.	(Cup ear with hands, then fold hands.)
Yes, He hears my prayer.	(Cup ear with hands, then fold hands.)
Oh, He hears my prayer.	(Cup ear with hands, then fold hands.)
When I pray, I'm talking to God,	(Fold hands, then point to heaven.)
And He hears my prayer.	(Cup ear with hands, then fold hands.)

For More Fun:

Make a class Big Book of Prayer. Give each child a sheet of paper. Let him or her dictate a simple prayer to you. (You might provide a prayer starter.) The children can decorate their pages. Assemble them and let each child "read" his or her page. (Examples of children's prayers: "Thank You, God, for my family." "Dear God, please help me be good today." "Please bless my friends, dear Father.")

Talking to God

God loves when we pray to Him. Connect the dots to see who prayed a lot to His Father in heaven. Color the picture.

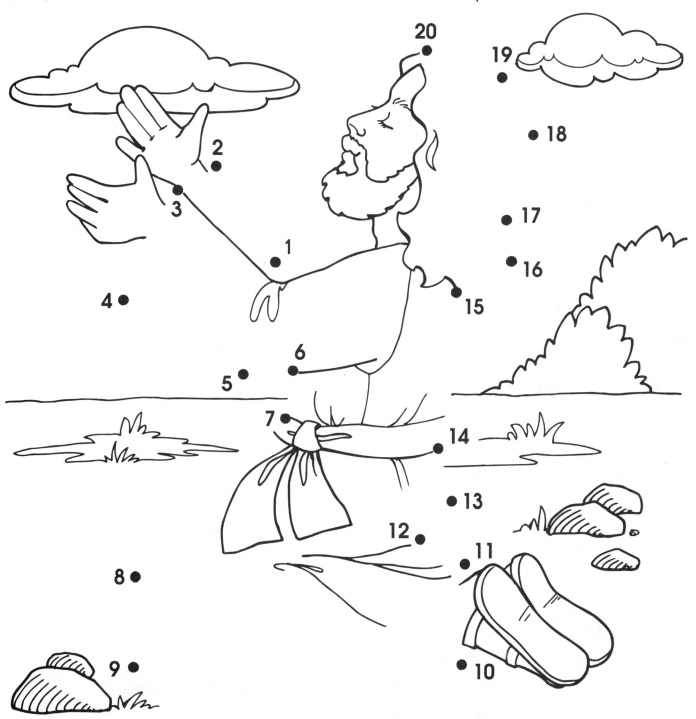

Jesus talked to God about everything.

SS48831

Where Can We Pray?

Some children have not been taught to pray at home by their parents. They may think that church is the only place to pray. Talk with the children about where we can pray. Make sure the children understand that we can talk to God wherever we are. Give each child a copy of page 7. Talk about each picture with the children.

Picture 1: Look at the first picture on your page. Where are the children? (on the playground, possibly at school) Can you pray on the playground? (Let the children share their ideas.) When you're playing, God is with you, so you can talk to Him there. He loves for us to talk to Him when we're having a good time.

Picture 2: Look at the picture of the church. Can we pray at church? (Yes. God loves for us to talk to Him in Sunday school and at church.) We might all pray together, or we might all close our eyes and listen as the pastor prays. Church is a very good place to pray. But it's not the only place we should pray.

Picture 3: Look at the picture of the family in their home. What are they doing? Do you think God likes for us to pray at home? When do you pray at your house? (Children may say "before meals" and "at bedtime.") We can pray to God whenever we want to at home. We can talk to Him when we're alone in our rooms, or we can whisper a short prayer when we're helping Mom, playing in the yard, or whatever we're doing.

Picture 4: Where is the family in the last picture? (on vacation) What are they doing? (camping) Do you think God likes for us to talk to Him when we're on vacation? Of course He does! No matter where we go—camping, shopping, to a park, or to see grandparents—we can talk to God. We can thank Him for the good time we're having and ask Him to help us do what He wants.

Where do you like to talk to God? (Let the children suggest places, such as in a playhouse, in my room, in the car, etc.) Remember the story of Jonah? He prayed from inside a fish! Paul and Silas prayed when they were in prison. Yes, we can talk to God anywhere, anytime. Let's talk to Him right now.

Lord,

Thank You for always being with us.

Thank You for always hearing us when we talk to You wherever we are.

Amen.

After you have discussed the pictures with the children and prayed, let the children color the pictures and cut them apart. The children can make a cover for their books, showing themselves praying somewhere. Help the children assemble the pages using yarn, ribbon, or a stapler.

Any Place, Any Time

We can talk to God any place, any time, and He will hear us. Look at the pictures. Where are the people? Can they talk to God where they are? Color the pictures.

I Can Pray Everywhere!

Draw a background to show where the little girl is praying. Maybe she is in her bedroom, at church, or in the yard.

When Should We Pray?

Explain to the children that the Bible has a lot to say about when we should pray. Many of the psalms are examples of when to pray.

Psalm 5   Pray when you need help.

Psalm 6   Pray when you are sad or don't feel well.

Psalm 9   Pray when you are happy and thankful.

Psalm 22   Pray when you need forgiveness because you have sinned.

Psalm 31   Pray when you are afraid.

Then tell the children that any time is the right time to talk to God. They don't have to wait until they have something to ask Him for. He wants them to talk to Him whenever they want to, even if it's just to tell Him how they are feeling. Tell the children that they don't have to wait until they are in church, or it's time for a meal, or it's time to go to bed. They can pray in the middle of the night. Ask the children if they have ever had a bad dream that woke them up and they couldn't get back to sleep. Tell them that this is a great time to talk to God. They can pray when they feel lonely or when they don't know what to do. They can even pray when they are angry. No matter what time it is, God is with us and ready to listen.

Teach the children the rhyme below. Say it together. Tell them that it will help them remember that they can pray anytime.

Tick tock, tick tock,
What time is it?
Time to talk to God,
To pay Him a visit.

One o'clock, two o'clock,
Almost three!
Anytime at all,
God loves to hear from me.

Bulletin Board Idea

Attach the title "When Should We Pray?" to a bulletin board. Have the children cut out pictures from magazines depicting times and places when people could pray. Let each child tell about his or her picture. Attach them to the board.

Time to Pray

Make a copy of the circles below and on page 11 on heavy paper for each child. Cut them out. Discuss the pictures with the children. Ask the children if they talk to God when they are feeling like the children in the pictures. Then have them color the pictures. Help each child attach the two circles together with a brad, putting the one with the pictures on the bottom. Show the children how to turn the bottom circle to reveal each picture as a reminder of when they can pray.

I pray . . .

Cut out.

Any time
is a good
time
to pray!

Prayer Wheel Pattern

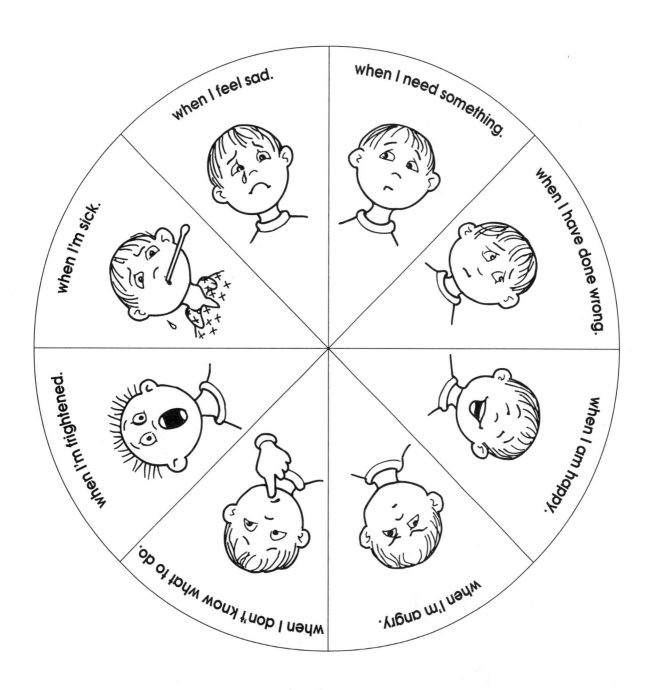

SS48831

How Should We Pray?

Most young children are taught to pray with folded hands, bowed head, and closed eyes. Encourage them to continue doing these things, but also help them understand that we can talk to God in other positions, too.

Give each child a copy of the pictures below. Ask the children what the children in the three pictures are doing. (praying or perhaps going to pray) Ask them why they think the children are praying or about to pray. (because they are kneeling, have heads down, have hands folded, are going to church with their parents, etc.) Tell the children that closing their eyes, kneeling, bowing their heads, and folding their hands helps us think only about God when we pray. This is a good way to pray. Then tell the children that they can also pray while they are riding a bike, running, walking with their parents, sitting in the dentist's office, etc. A prayer can be as simple as saying, "Hello, Jesus!" Talk about different ways other people pray. (lying down, with hands raised, holding hands with others, etc.) Have each child draw a picture of himself or herself praying in the empty box. The children can cut apart the pictures and assemble them to create little books.

When the children are done coloring, have them all hold hands and say this prayer:

Dear Father, Thank You for letting us talk to You with our eyes open or closed, sitting down or kneeling. We love You. Amen.

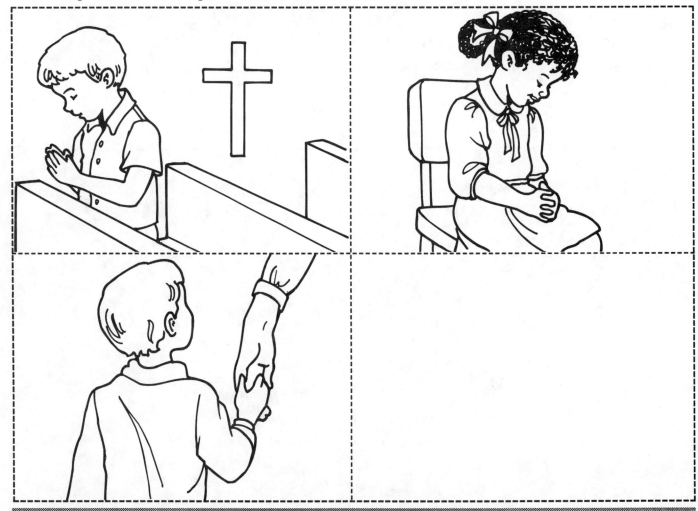

Matching Game

Look carefully at the ways we can pray below. Two pictures in each row are exactly alike. Color them.

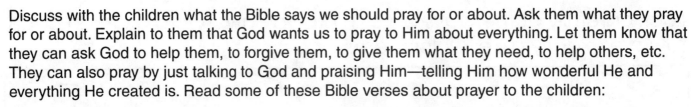

What Should We Pray for?

Discuss with the children what the Bible says we should pray for or about. Ask them what they pray for or about. Explain to them that God wants us to pray to Him about everything. Let them know that they can ask God to help them, to forgive them, to give them what they need, to help others, etc. They can also pray by just talking to God and praising Him—telling Him how wonderful He and everything He created is. Read some of these Bible verses about prayer to the children:

Psalm 92 (Pray to praise God.)   Matthew 5:43–44 (Pray for our enemies.)

Philippians 4:6 (Pray about problems.)   1 John 1:9 (Pray for forgiveness.)

Give each child a copy of the boxes below. The children can complete each sentence with a picture.

Thank You, God, for . . .	Dear God, I'm sorry for . . .
Dear Father, please help me . . .	Oh Lord, You are wonderful because You . . .

Prayer Bulletin Board

What should I say to God?

Jack

I love you.

Sandie

Help me.

Ashly

Megan

Kyle

Forgive me.

Andrew

Give me what I need.

Chris

Help that person.

Thank you.

Tyler

Tasha

I can talk to Him about everything!

Children will enjoy helping you assemble this special bulletin board to illustrate what we should pray for or about.

Directions:

1. Make a copy of the praying child pattern to the left and color it. (You may want to enlarge it, depending on the size of your board.) Attach it to the center of the board.

2. Use a thick marker to write "What Should I Say to God?" and "I can talk to Him about everything!" on long strips of paper. Attach them to the top and bottom of the board.

3. Use a marker to write the sentences featured on the board (see above) on rectangles of colored paper. Add any others you or the children want. Let the children attach them to the board around the picture.

4. Trace each child's hand, fingers together, on a piece of paper. Let the children color their hands. Print the name of each child on his or her hand and cut it out. Let the children attach these to the board.

Who Should We Pray for?

I can pray for everyone!

Ask the children who they pray for. Let the children share names. Tell them that there are so many people we can pray for—ourselves, moms and dads, brothers and sisters, friends, neighbors, the leaders of our country, people we know who are sick or sad or in need, people who don't know Jesus, and so many others!

Play a game to help the children think of some people they can pray for. Tell the children that you will say a letter of the alphabet, and they should try to think of someone whose name starts with that letter that they can pray for. For example, you say, "The first letter is **A**. **A** reminds me that I can pray for my Aunt Alice. The second letter is **B**. Can you think of someone whose name starts with the letter **B** that you can pray for?" You may need to help the children with some of the letters. Some people may be mentioned by title, such as **B** for bus driver, rather than by name. Go as far through the alphabet as possible.

After the game, have a brief time of prayer. Have each child pray for the child seated on his or her right. (You will have to point this out for the children since many children will not know their right from their left.) Ask the children to pray aloud. Close by asking God to bless everyone in the group.

Let the children make mini prayer booklets. To do this, make a copy of pages 17–18 and a copy of the cover to the right for each child. Cut the boxes apart on the dotted lines and have the children complete the features, add hair, and color their pictures. Staple the pages together after the children are done coloring them. Go over each page together. Encourage the children to take them home and use them as reminders of who to pray for.

I Can Pray for . . .

Mini Prayer Booklet

I can pray for . . .

myself.

1

I can pray for . . .

my pastor.

2

I can pray for . . .

my friends.

3

I can pray for . . .

my cousins.

4

SS48831

I can pray for . . .

my family. 5

I can pray for . . .

sick people. 6

I can pray for . . .

hungry people. 7

I can pray for . . .

sad people. 8

SS48831

I Can Pray for . . .

God loves to hear us pray to Him for others, especially people who are sick or hurt. Circle the picture in each box showing who you would pray for most.

A Servant's Prayer

Based on Genesis 24

Read the story below to the children. Then ask the children the questions that follow.

Abraham was an old man. His son, Isaac, was old enough to get married, but Abraham was worried about him. He was afraid Isaac might decide to marry one of the local girls who were idol worshippers. Abraham wanted his son to have a wife who loved God, so he spoke to his most trusted servant about it. "I want you to go back to the land I came from to find a wife for my son."

"What if the woman doesn't want to come back here with me?" asked the servant. "Shall I take Isaac back there to marry her?"

"No," said Abraham. "Don't take my son back there. God will work it out so that you find just the right wife for Isaac, and she'll come here."

The servant promised to do what Abraham asked. He took 10 camels loaded with all kinds of good things and headed for the area his master had come from. He stopped near a well at the town of Nahor in the early evening. This was the time when women came to the well to get water every day.

The servant prayed, "Lord, give me success today. Help me to do what my master asked of me. I will ask one of these women coming for water to give me a drink. If she says she will not only give me a drink, but will water my camels also, I will know that the woman is the one You have chosen for Isaac."

When the servant looked up, he saw a pretty girl named Rebekah getting water in a large jar. He hurried over to her and said, "May I please have a drink of your water?"

Rebekah gave him a drink. Then she said, "I'll get water for your camels to drink, too." And she did.

Abraham's servant thought this must be the girl God wanted Isaac to marry. He was sure of it when he asked her about her family and discovered that she was actually related to Abraham! He bowed down and thanked the Lord for leading him to the right wife for Isaac. Then he went to Rebekah's home and met her family. He told them why he had come. Everyone agreed that this was the Lord's work. Rebekah agreed to go back with the servant to become Isaac's wife.

When Rebekah and Abraham's servant got near home, Rebekah saw Isaac coming to meet them. Isaac loved her, and they were married. Abraham's servant thanked God for answering his prayer and helping him do what his master had asked of him.

Questions for Discussion:
- Who prayed for something? *(servant)*
- What did he pray for? *(success in finding a wife for Isaac)*
- What do you think Abraham prayed for?
- What do you think Rebekah prayed for?

Hidden Camels

Abraham's servant asked Rebekah for a drink. She gave it to him. She offered to water his camels, too. This was an answer to his prayer. Find the 10 camels hidden in the picture.

Give Me a Son!

Based on 1 Samuel 1:1–28

Practice saying the poem below until you can say it
by memory or with just a few notes. As you say it, act
out some of the parts, such as kneeling down when
Hannah prays and standing up with arms
outstretched in blessing when Eli talks to Hannah.
Ask the children the questions that follow.

There once was a woman named Hannah who badly wanted a son.

She didn't have any children—no, not even one.

She prayed to the Lord, "Please help me! Give me a son; please do!

I promise I'll raise him to worship and honor only You!"

She silently cried out to God as tears ran down her face.

Eli, the priest, wondered, "What's she doing in this place?

I see her lips are moving, but no sound is coming out.

Is the woman very sick? It's strange, without a doubt."

Hannah spoke to Eli. She told him, "I'm so sad.

I'm asking God for a son. A son would make me glad!

I'm sorry I disturbed you. I was very upset, you see.

I was crying because I want so much for God to answer me."

Eli said to Hannah, "Go in peace. And I pray

That the God of Israel may give you what you have asked for today."

God answered Hannah's prayer and gave her a baby boy.

She named her child Samuel. Now Hannah was full of joy.

When he was a little older, Hannah took Samuel to stay

With Eli, the priest, to help him and serve the Lord every day.

Hannah missed her son, but she'd promised to give Him back to the Lord.

God had answered her prayer, and she knew she must keep her word.

So Samuel grew up in the Lord's house and learned to serve God there

Because Hannah had prayed for a son, and God had answered her prayer.

Questions for Discussion:

• Who prayed for something? *(Hannah and Eli)*

• What did Hannah pray for? *(a baby boy)*

• What did Eli pray about? *(that God would answer Hannah's prayer)*

• How did God answer Hannah's prayer? *(He gave her a son.)*

Samuel Meets Eli

Hannah asked God for a son. She promised to give him back to God. God answered her prayer. When she grew older, Hannah took young Samuel to Eli, the priest, so he could serve the Lord.

Color the picture. Cut on the lines. Put the pieces back together.

A Shepherd's Prayer

Based on 1 Samuel 16:23, 17:34–37

Read the children the story below. Then ask them the questions that follow. If you have a children's version of Psalm 23, read and discuss it with the children.

David wasn't always a king. When he was a boy, David was the shepherd for his family's sheep. He went out with them to the fields. He made sure they had fresh green grass to eat and clean water to drink. He poured oil on sheep that got injured or had sores on their bodies. The oil was like medicine to make them well. David protected his sheep from danger, too. He once killed a lion that grabbed a young sheep. Another time, he killed a bear that wanted to eat one of his sheep.

David was a good shepherd, but he knew someone who was a Great Shepherd—God! As his sheep grazed all day, David often sat on a rock or under a tree and played his harp. He made up songs of praise to God and sang them. As he took care of his sheep, David thought how people are like sheep and God is like a Shepherd, taking care of His flock. David wrote a love song to God, thanking Him for His care.

Questions for Discussion:

• What did David probably pray for?

• How did David pray to God? *(He made up songs of praise and sang them.)*

• If you were a shepherd, what would you pray for?

Give each child a copy of the picture below. The children can color the picture and glue cotton balls on the sheep.

The Lord is my Shepherd.

Help Me!

Uh oh! David can't find five sheep! Help David find his sheep.
Circle them.

A Prayer for Wisdom

Based on 1 Kings 3:3–15

As you tell the story below, pantomime Solomon's actions as he becomes sleepy, goes to bed, falls asleep, has a dream, and wakes up. Let the children copy your actions. Then discuss the questions below.

David's son, Solomon, became king after David died. He wanted to be a good king like his father had been. He wanted to help people follow the Lord and obey His Word.

One day, King Solomon went to a special place to make a thousand burnt offerings to God. At the end of the day, Solomon was very tired. He was so sleepy. *(Yawn and stretch.)* He lay down on his bed. *(Lie down on the floor or rest your head on folded hands and lean against something.)* He closed his eyes. *(Close your eyes.)* He was soon fast asleep. *(Snore gently.)*

As Solomon slept, he had a wonderful dream. In his dream, God spoke to him. "Ask me for anything you want, and I'll give it to you," God said to him.

Wow! What would Solomon ask for—a beautiful palace, thousands of horses, lots of money? No, King Solomon didn't ask for any of those things. He wanted only one thing from God. He knew that being king was going to be a very hard job, so Solomon asked God for wisdom. "Give me an understanding heart," he said to God, "and help me to be able to always know right from wrong."

God was pleased with Solomon's request. In fact, He was so pleased, He not only promised to give Solomon the wisdom he had asked for, but God also promised to give him more wisdom than anyone had ever had before! And God promised to give Solomon what he had not asked for—great riches and honor.

Suddenly, Solomon woke up! *(Raise your head, look around as if confused, and stretch.)* Why, it had been a dream! It had seemed so real. Had God really spoken to him and promised him great wisdom?

Yes, it was real. And God kept His promise. Solomon was king for 40 years. And he was so rich and famous, people came from all over the world to meet him and see his kingdom.

Questions for Discussion:

- What did Solomon pray to God for? *(an understanding heart; to always know right from wrong)*
- Was God happy that Solomon prayed for those things? *(yes)*
- How do you know this? *(because God also gave Solomon riches and honor)*
- Do you pray to God to help you do right?

Solomon Paper Doll

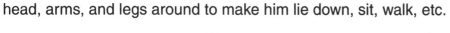

Make a copy of the patterns below on heavy paper for each child to color. Help the children cut out the pieces and put them together with small brad fasteners. Show them how to move Solomon's head, arms, and legs around to make him lie down, sit, walk, etc.

SS48831

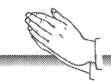

I Do the Right Thing

We need to pray to God to do the right thing. Color the pictures of the children doing the right things.

A Prayer With a Promise

Based on 2 Kings 22–23

Tell the story of Josiah using the stick puppets made from page 30. Then let the children make their own puppets to act out the story. Encourage them to take their puppets home and use them to tell the story to their families. Discuss the questions that follow the story with the children.

Can you imagine being an eight-year-old king? That's how old Josiah was when he became king. *(Hold up young Josiah.)* Of course, he couldn't do much on his own. He had to listen to adults and follow their advice. But there was one thing he knew to do all on his own—obey God and be an example to his people by serving God.

When Josiah grew up, he was able to begin making his own decisions for his people. *(Hold up older Josiah.)* One of his decisions was to repair God's temple. It needed a lot of work done on it, and money had been collected to fix it up.

One day when some men were working on the temple, someone found an old book. The priest was excited! It wasn't just any old book—it was the Book of the Law—God's Word! *(Hold up the priest. Tape the Book of the Law to his hands.)* He gave it to the king's secretary, who read part of it to Josiah.

King Josiah was so upset, he began tearing his robe. "We have not been obeying God's Word," he said. The book told what God wanted His people to do, and they had not been doing it.

King Josiah ordered all the people and their leaders to meet at the temple. He read aloud from the Book of the Law. *(Tape the Book of the Law to Josiah's hands.)* He wanted everyone to hear what God wanted them to do. Then Josiah promised the Lord that he and the people would obey the commands in the Book of the Law. He pledged that he would lead God's people in following the Lord, and the people pledged that they would follow.

Josiah started making changes right away. He told the priests to remove the idols the people had been worshipping and burn them. He did everything he could to get rid of anything connected with idol worship in the land. He commanded that everyone should start celebrating Passover again. No one had remembered the Passover celebration for years and years, but now they would have it every year.

The Bible says there was never a king who turned to the Lord like Josiah with all his heart and soul and strength! Josiah made a promise to obey God, and he kept his promise.

Questions for Discussion:

- Josiah was good because he read God's Word and listened to what it said. How have you been good today?
- How can you show God you love Him with all your heart?
- Josiah helped his people follow God's law. How can you follow God's law?

Josiah Stick Puppets

Copy the patterns below on heavy paper for each child to color and cut out. Provide tongue depressors or strips of heavy cardboard the children can glue on the back of each puppet. Roll up a small piece of tape to attach the Book of the Law to the priest's hands and then to Josiah's hands.

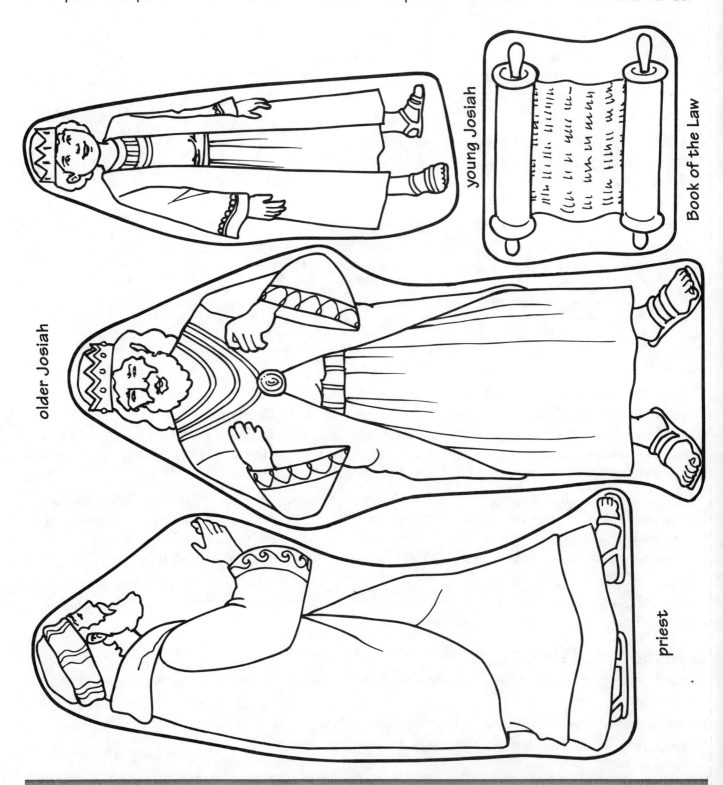

young Josiah

Book of the Law

older Josiah

priest

A Prayer for Forgiveness

Based on Jonah 1–3

To make the story of Jonah come alive for the children, cut out as large a fish shape as possible from cardboard or an old sheet. It should have an open mouth. Hang the fish at the front of the room. As you tell about Jonah being swallowed by the fish, walk behind the hanging fish as if you are inside it. Poke your head out to continue the story. When Jonah is spit out of the fish, come out from behind the fish. After the story, let the children pretend to go in and out of the fish. Ask the children the questions for discussion at the bottom of the page.

God had a special job for Jonah. He wanted Jonah to go to a special city. Jonah was to tell the people there to stop being bad. But Jonah didn't want to go. He decided to run away from God. He got on a ship and tried to run away from God.

While Jonah was on the ship, a terrible storm came up. The wind blew, and the waves of the sea rocked the ship back and forth. The men in charge of the ship thought it was going to sink. They thought they would all drown! They began throwing things overboard to lighten the ship, but that didn't help.

The captain woke Jonah and told him to pray to his God to keep them from drowning. Jonah realized right away what was causing the storm—him! He told the captain and his men, "I worship the God who made the sea and everything else. I am running away from Him, so He has caused this storm to stop me."

"What are we going to do?" asked the men.

"You must throw me into the sea," Jonah told them, "and it will calm down."

The men didn't want to throw Jonah overboard, so they kept trying to control the ship and get it to land. But finally, they had to do what Jonah had told them. They picked him up and threw him into the churning sea. Immediately, the wind and water calmed down. The storm was over.

God was watching over Jonah and didn't let him drown. Instead, Jonah was swallowed by a huge fish! Inside the fish, Jonah was still alive, and he prayed to God. "Forgive me, Lord. I know I've done wrong, but I will obey You from now on." God heard Jonah's prayer and answered him.

Jonah was inside that fish for three days and nights. Then God made the fish spit Jonah out on dry land! He didn't even have to swim to shore! God told Jonah again what He wanted him to do. This time, Jonah did it. He headed for the city where God wanted him to preach to the people about Him. The people of the city listened to Jonah and put their faith in God.

Jonah is the only person who ever prayed for forgiveness from inside a fish! And even in that strange place, God heard him and forgave him.

Questions for Discussion:

- What do you think Jonah prayed for when he was in the fish?
- What would you pray for if you were swallowed by a fish?
- When there is a bad storm outside, what can you pray to God for?

Prayer Plaque

Make a copy of the picture below and the figure of Jonah to the right on heavy paper for each child to color. Let each child cut out Jonah and glue him inside the fish. Then hand out blue and black or gray yarn. Put glue around the fish outline and the sea waves. Show the children how to put the black or gray yarn on the glue around the fish and the blue yarn on the waves. Encourage the children to take their pictures home and hang them up as prayer reminders.

God hears our prayers wherever we are.

SS48831

Daniel Thanks God

Based on Daniel 2

Read the children the story below. Then ask them the questions for discussion.

King Nebuchadnezzar was having strange dreams. He was having trouble sleeping, wondering what the dreams meant. Finally, he called some of his wise men and some magicians to him. "I want you to explain my dreams," he told them.

"Of course, king," they replied. "Just tell us what you dreamed, and we'll explain them."

"Oh no," said the king. "First you must tell me what I dreamed; then tell me what they mean."

"We can't do that!" the wise men and magicians cried. "How can we tell what you dreamed?"

"Then you shall all die!" yelled the king in anger. And he sent his soldiers out to find all the wise men in the country so they could kill them.

Daniel met one of the soldiers and asked him what was happening. When the soldier explained, Daniel went to see King Nebuchadnezzar. He asked the king to give him a little time, and he would tell the king about his dreams. The king agreed.

Daniel immediately asked his friends, Shadrach, Meshach, and Abednego, to pray with him, asking God to reveal the king's dreams to him. They prayed together, and that night, God showed Daniel the dreams and what they meant.

Daniel prayed again, thanking God for His help. "You are the One who gives wisdom and understanding," Daniel prayed. "Thank You for answering our prayers."

Then Daniel went to the soldier in charge of killing all the wise men. "Do not kill any of them yet," Daniel said to him. "Take me to the king, and I will tell him what he wants to know."

The soldier took him to Nebuchadnezzar. The king said to Daniel, "Are you indeed able to tell me what I dreamed and what it meant?"

Daniel replied, "No man is wise enough to do that, your highness. Only God can, and He has revealed to me the secrets of your dreams. In your dreams, God has been showing you what will happen in the future."

The king listened quietly as Daniel told him what he had dreamed and explained what it all meant. Daniel made it very clear that the king's dreams were from God, so Nebuchadnezzar should pay attention to them.

When Daniel finished talking, King Nebuchadnezzar bowed before him and said, . . . *"Surely your God is the God of gods and the Lord of kings and a revealer of mysteries . . ."* (Daniel 2:47) Then the king gave Daniel expensive gifts and a very important job, putting him in charge of all the wise men in the land. Daniel told the king about his three friends who had prayed with him, and they were also given important jobs.

Questions for Discussion:

- What did Daniel and his three friends pray to God for about the king's dreams? *(They wanted to know what the dreams were and what they meant.)*
- Did God answer Daniel and his friends' prayers? *(yes)*
- Was the king happy that Daniel knew what his dreams meant? *(yes)*
- What did you dream about last night?

A Thankfulness Reminder

Make a copy of this page and page 35 for each child. Cut out the two circles for each child. Let each child choose five of the things pictured for which to thank God, color them, and cut them out. Help each child glue his or her pictures on the circle that is divided into five sections. Attach the top circle to the picture circle at the center with a brad fastener. Show the children how to turn the top circle to show each thing to help them remember what to thank God for.

Cut out.

Thank You, Lord, for all these things.

SS48831

A Thankfulness . . . continued

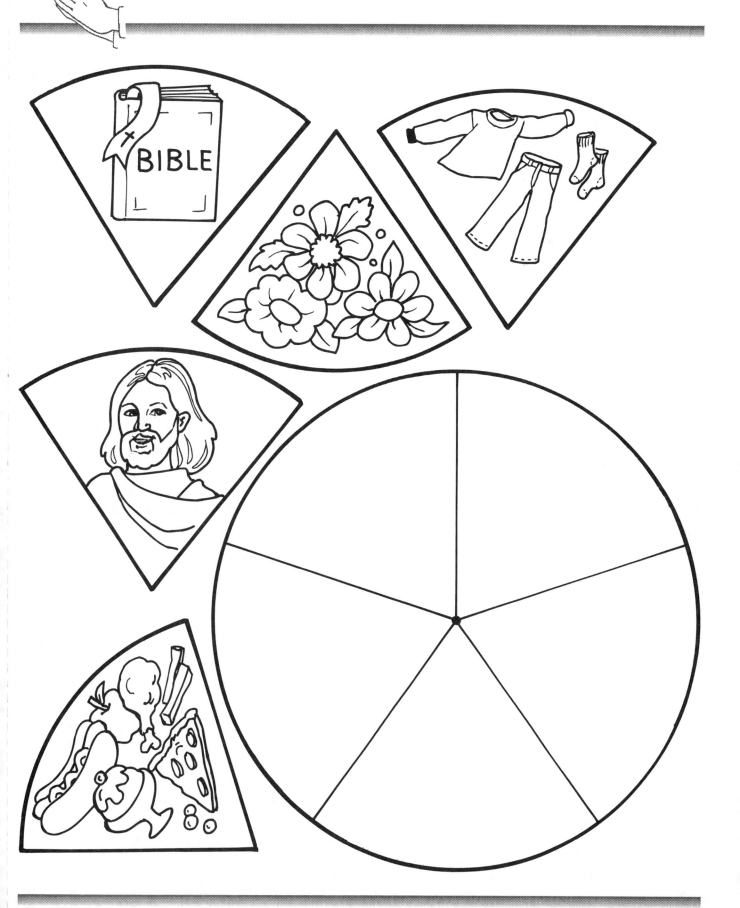

A Prayer Meeting for Peter

Based on Acts 12

Make the craft on page 37 and use it to capture the children's attention for the story below. Hold it up with Peter behind bars, then unfold it to take Peter out of prison at the appropriate time in the story. After the story and the questions for discussion, give each child a copy of the craft to make and take home.

Peter was in prison. He had done nothing wrong, but King Herod had arrested him because he knew it would please some people. Many people didn't like the way Peter and his friends preached about Jesus.

The king was taking no chances that Peter would escape. He had him guarded by four squads of soldiers with four men in each squad. That's 16 soldiers with swords to guard one man! Peter was never left alone. Even when he was sleeping, he was bound with two chains between two soldiers. There was no way he could escape!

Peter's Christian friends met in each other's homes to pray together. One night, they were praying together at the home of Mary, John's mother. That night, their prayers were answered.

Peter was sleeping when someone woke him up. It was an angel that God had sent to get him out of prison. "Get up!" said the angel, and the chains fell off of Peter's wrists. The guards he was chained to didn't even wake up! The angel told him to get dressed. Then the angel began to lead Peter out of the prison right past all the soldiers standing guard! The angel took him outside the prison to the city gate. The gate opened by itself, and Peter and the angel walked through. Peter was free!

Peter and the angel walked down the street, and suddenly the angel was gone. Peter looked around him. It had felt like a dream, but there he was, outside the prison. "Now I know that the Lord sent His angel to rescue me," he said. Then he hurried to Mary's house.

Peter knocked on the door. A servant girl was about to open it when she heard Peter's voice. She was so excited, she forgot to open the door, but ran into the room where Peter's friends were praying. "Peter's at the door!" she cried.

"That can't be!" someone said. "You must be imagining things." But they finally went to the door. All this time, Peter had been knocking. They opened the door, and there stood Peter! Everyone realized that God had answered their prayers far better than they had expected—with a miracle!

Questions for Discussion:

• What did Peter probably pray for when he was in jail?
• What were Peter's friends probably praying for?
• What did Peter probably say to God for helping him get out of jail?
• What would you say to God if you were in jail?

In and Out of Prison

Give each child a copy of the rectangle below. Have the children color Peter. Then have them cut on the dotted lines and glue on four bars made from black construction paper. The children can fold on the center line to show Peter in prison and unfold to show Peter freed from prison.

Cut out this center rectangle along the dotted lines. Glue four ¼" x 7" strips of black construction paper as shown above.

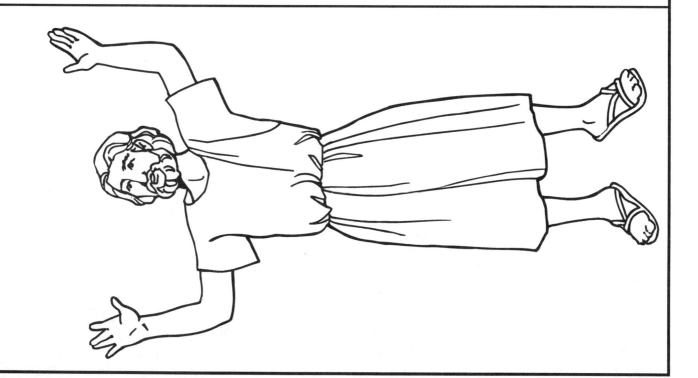

The Lord's Prayer

Based on Matthew 6:5–15

Tell the children the story below. Then lead the children in singing the song which puts into their language the main points of Jesus' sample prayer.

One day, Jesus took His disciples up on a mountainside to teach them some important lessons. He talked to them about everyday concerns, such as obeying God, loving others, and sharing what they had with needy people. Then He began to talk to them about prayer. He said, "When you pray, do it quietly, not loudly where everybody can hear you. Prayer is talking to God, not trying to impress people."

"Pray like this," Jesus said . . ."*Our Father in heaven, hallowed be your name, your kingdom come, your will be done on earth as it is in heaven. Give us today our daily bread. Forgive us our debts, as we also have forgiven our debtors. And lead us not into temptation, but deliver us from the evil one.'*" (Matthew 6:9–13)

In some churches, people repeat this prayer every Sunday. But Jesus didn't mean we should just repeat that prayer over and over. He meant that whenever we talk to God, we should include those ideas in our prayers: praising Him, thanking Him, asking Him to provide what we need, confessing our sins and asking for forgiveness, and asking Him to help us obey Him every day.

Teach the children the prayer song below that includes each of the things we need to say to God.

(Tune: "This Is the Way We Wash Our Clothes")

This is the way we pray to God,
Pray to God, pray to God.
This is the way we pray to God,
Each and every day.

Thank You, God, for what You do,
What You do, what You do.
Thank You, God, for what You do,
Each and every day.

We love You, God, for who You are,
Who You are, who You are.
We love You, God, for who You are,
Each and every day.

Give us what we need today,
Need today, need today.
Give us what we need today,
Each and every day.

Forgive us for the wrong we've done,
Wrong we've done, wrong we've done.
Forgive us for the wrong we've done,
Each and every day.

Help us to obey Your Word,
Obey Your Word, obey Your Word.
Help us to obey Your Word,
Each and every day.

Prayer Pin

Make a copy of the circle below on heavy paper or posterboard for each child and cut it out. Let each child choose one of the symbols below to put on his or her pin. Have the children color their symbols and then glue them to the circles. Glue a pin to the back of each circle or attach a paper clip. Pin them to the children's shirts or clip them onto a pocket or collar.

I love to talk to God!

"I Love You" Prayers

Lead the children in saying the prayer below and doing the actions. Read Psalm 139 aloud from a children's version of the Bible and talk about how God knows everything about us and still loves us. This prayer gives children a chance to express their love for Him, too.

Lord, You Know Me
(Based on Psalm 139)

Lord, You know me.	*(Clap, clap, clap.)*
And You're watching over me,	
When I'm sitting,	*(Sit down.)*
When I'm standing,	*(Stand up.)*
When I'm lying down to sleep.	*(Pretend to sleep.)*
Lord, You know me.	*(Clap, clap, clap.)*
And You care about me, too.	*(Point to heaven, then to self.)*
You know everything I think or say and everything I do.	
Lord, You know me.	*(Clap, clap, clap.)*
And You love me.	*(Point to heaven, then to self.)*
And I	*(Point to self.)*
Love You!	*(Raise arms toward heaven.)*

The song below is fun for the children to sing and to add on to. Let them suggest additional words to personalize this prayer.

I Love You, Lord
(Tune: "God Is So Good")

I love You, Lord,
For You are good.
I love You, Lord, for You're good to me.

I love You, Lord,
For You made me.
I love You, Lord, for You made me.

I love You, Lord.
You hear my prayers.
I love You, Lord, for You hear my prayers.

I love You, Lord.
Your Word is true.
I love You, Lord, for Your Word is true.

I love You, Lord.
You love me, too.
I love You, Lord, for You love me, too.

"Thank You" Prayers

A Counting Prayer

As the children say the prayer below, have them count on their fingers and then wave both hands around with all fingers extended on "10."

1-2-3—Father, You love me.

4-5-6—There's nothing You can't fix!

7-8-9—You're with me all the time.

10-10-10—You are my best friend!

Thank You

Before you teach the children the prayer below, ask them to tell what they are thankful for. Many will probably answer with some of the things mentioned in the prayer. This sharing time will help prepare them for mentioning things for which they want to thank God in the prayer.

Thank You for my family
And friends who mean so much to me.
Thank You for my home where I'm
Taken care of all the time.
Thank You for my neighbors who
Welcome and encourage, too.
Thank You for my church, dear Lord,
Where I learn about Your Word.
There's so much to thank You for.
Here are just a few things more:
(Let the children share things for which they want to thank God.)
Thanks for every single one,
And thanks especially for Your Son.
In Jesus' name,
Amen.

A "Thank You, God" Bulletin Board

Attach the title "Thank You, God, for . . ." to a bulletin board. Let the children draw or cut out pictures of things for which they are thankful and attach them to the board.

Prayers continued

"Thank You" Prayer

After each stanza of this song, stop to ask the children a question.

Let Us Pray
(Tune: "London Bridge")

Let us pray and thank the Lord,
Thank the Lord, thank the Lord.
Let us pray and thank the Lord.
Thank You, Father.

Question: *What would you like to thank God for?*

Let us thank Him for His Son,
For His Son, for His Son.
Let us thank Him for His Son.
Thank You, Father.

Question: *Who is God's Son? (Jesus)*

Let us thank Him for His care,
For His care, for His care.
Let us thank Him for His care.
Thank You, Father.

Question: *In what ways does the Lord take care of us? (provides for our needs, protects us, answers our prayers, etc.)*

Let us thank Him as we pray,
As we learn and obey.
Let us thank Him every day.
Thank You, Father.

Questions: *How can we learn more about God? (by going to Sunday school and church) Will you show Him you're thankful by obeying His Word?*

Let us pray and thank the Lord,
Thank the Lord, thank the Lord.
Let us pray and thank the Lord.
Thank You, Father.

"Forgive Me" Prayer

As you say this prayer, have the children repeat each line after you and silently fill in the blank with whatever they need to confess to the Lord.

Dear Lord,
I want to be good and do what You say,
But sometimes I'm not, and I disobey.
I know that You love me no matter what I do,
But my sin makes You sad, and it hurts me, too.
Forgive me, dear Lord, and please help me
To be the child You want me to be.
Forgive me for _____.
In the name of Jesus, my very best friend,
I pray this prayer. Thank You and Amen.

"Help Me" Prayers

A Shining Light

After singing this prayer song with the children, have a brief discussion, using the questions below.

(Tune: "Twinkle, Twinkle, Little Star")

Father, help me do what's right
And to be a shining light
To my friends and family,
So they'll see that You love me,
And You love them, every one.
That is why You sent Your Son.

Questions for Discussion:

• How can you be a shining light for the Lord? *(by obeying, helping cheerfully, telling others about Jesus)*

• Why did God send His Son, Jesus, to earth? *(to show His love for people; He died for people's sins.)*

An A-B-C Prayer

Since preschoolers are proud to show that they can say some (or all) of the alphabet, they'll enjoy this prayer and remember it.

A-B-C-D-E-F-G—Father, won't You please help me.
H-I-J-K-L-M-N—Help me be a loving friend.
O-P-Q-R-S-T-U—Show me, Lord, what I can do
V-W-X-Y-Z—To share the love that You give me.

A Sharing Prayer

This prayer is a good one to help children begin each day with a goal in mind!

Dear Lord,
I quietly kneel and close my eyes and fold my hands in prayer,
To say, "Don't let me be selfish today. Father, please help me to share."

"Please Give Me" Prayers

God Provides

And my God will meet all your needs according to his glorious riches in Christ Jesus.
(Philippians 4:19) Sing the song below together. Then ask the children what they need each day to live. Point out the difference between things we really need and things we just want.

(Tune: "Row, Row, Row Your Boat")
Lord, I know that You will provide for me—
Food and water, clothes and home—Everything I need.

Give Me Satisfaction

After you say the prayer below together, ask the children if they know what it means to be satisfied. *(to be happy with the way things are)* Ask them if they are happy with what God has given them—their family, home, clothes, toys, etc.

Give me, dear Lord, what You want me to have,
And make me satisfied.
Help me not to complain if it's not what I want,
And be glad that You're by my side.

A Prayer to Care

Talk about ways the children can help and encourage others. Then say the prayer below together.

Dear Lord,
Give me a great big smile today   *(Smile with hands cupped around mouth to show off the smile.)*

To cheer up someone who's sad.
Give me arms that are ready to hug   *(Hug yourself.)*
Anyone who feels bad.
Give me a happy tune to sing   *(Clap hands and sing "la-la.")*
To encourage someone who's down.
Give me a kind word I can speak   *(Point to mouth.)*
To help erase someone's frown.
Make me a cheerful helper today   *(Hold out arms as far as they'll stretch.)*
To share Your love everywhere.
Give me, dear Lord, ways to show
Everyone that I care.   *(Go around the room smiling at everyone, hugging and saying kind things.)*

Praise Prayers

Praise the Lord Everyone!

Have children walk around in a circle as they sing the prayer below and do the actions. They should kneel down, bow their heads, and fold their hands on the last stanza.

(Tune: "If You're Happy and You Know It")

Praise the Lord, everyone, praise the Lord!	*(Clap, clap.)*
Praise the Lord, everyone, praise the Lord!	*(Clap, clap.)*
He created everything. Let your joyful praises ring!	
Praise the Lord, everyone, praise the Lord!	*(Clap, clap.)*
Praise the Lord, everyone, praise the Lord!	*(Stomp, stomp.)*
Praise the Lord, everyone, praise the Lord!	*(Stomp, stomp.)*
He sent His only Son to die for everyone.	
Praise the Lord, everyone, praise the Lord!	*(Stomp, stomp.)*
Praise the Lord, everyone, praise the Lord!	*(Hoo-ray!)*
Praise the Lord, everyone, praise the Lord!	*(Hoo-ray!)*
He's the greatest one of all, but He hears us when we call.	
Praise the Lord, everyone, praise the Lord!	*(Hoo-ray!)*
Praise the Lord, everyone, praise the Lord!	*(Amen.)*
Praise the Lord, everyone, praise the Lord!	*(Amen.)*
Let us kneel down to pray as we talk to Him today.	
Praise the Lord, everyone, praise the Lord!	*(Amen.)*

Little Children Praise

This tune is a favorite of many preschoolers. Teach them the words below.

(Tune: "I Will Make You Fishers of Men")

Even little children like me, children like me, children like me,

Even little children like me can praise You, Lord!

I can praise You, Lord! I can praise You, Lord!

Even little children like me can praise You, Lord!

Additional stanzas: Replace "praise" with "love" or "serve."

Praise Prayers continued

Creation Prayer

Let the children suggest their own lists of favorite things God has made in addition to the ones mentioned in the rhyming prayer below.

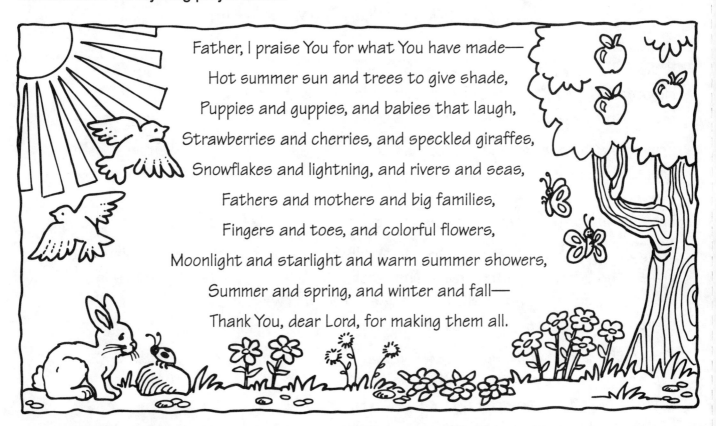

Father, I praise You for what You have made—
Hot summer sun and trees to give shade,
Puppies and guppies, and babies that laugh,
Strawberries and cherries, and speckled giraffes,
Snowflakes and lightning, and rivers and seas,
Fathers and mothers and big families,
Fingers and toes, and colorful flowers,
Moonlight and starlight and warm summer showers,
Summer and spring, and winter and fall—
Thank You, dear Lord, for making them all.

Praise the Lord (an echo prayer)

Divide the children into two groups with an adult leader or helper for each group. One group says a line of the prayer and the other group echoes it.

Group 1		Group 2 (Echo)	
Praise the Lord!	(loudly)	Praise the Lord!	(loudly)
Praise the Lord.	(softly)	Praise the Lord.	(softly)
He is good!	(a little louder)	He is good!	(a little louder)
He's our King!	(louder still)	He's our King!	(louder still)
Let us pray.	(softly)	Let us pray.	(softly)
Let us sing!	(loudly)	Let us sing!	(loudly)
Praise the Lord!	(loudly)	Praise the Lord!	(loudly)
Praise the Lord!	(together)	Praise the Lord!	(together)

Helping Others Prayers

A Prayer for Help

Sit in a circle with the children to share prayer requests. Ask them for the names of specific people they want to pray for. Sing the song below together several times, placing the name of a person and the request in the song each time. (Example: "Please help Jessie's dad find the job he needs.")

(Tune: "B-I-N-G-O")

We will pray and ask the Lord to help some special people.

Please help _____. Please help_____.

Please help_____ to _____.

A Prayer for the Sick

Teach the children to say this prayer, mentioning the names of sick people they know.

Dear Lord,

The Bible says that I should pray for people who are sick.

So here's my list of people. Please make them well real quick.

(names of sick people the child knows)

Thank You, Lord, for caring for every single one,

And for the love You have for them through Jesus Christ, Your Son.

Bless Them

Young children love to pray for people they love. This prayer is a simple one they can use to ask for God's blessing on their families, friends, neighbors, etc.

Lord,

Bless the people that I love.

Watch over them from up above.

Keep them well and safe from harm

Like lambs within the Shepherd's arms.

Amen.

Awards

_____

says
Perfectly Pleasing Prayers to God! God loves you!

_____
name

_____
date

_____

**knows how to
talk to God with
prayer! Keep talking!**

_____
name

_____
date